What He Hates

NAIDENE RALPH

What He Hates

Copyright © 2020 by Naidene Ralph

All rights reserved. No part of this publication may be reproduced, distributed, or transmitted in any form or by any means, including photocopying, recording, or other electronic or mechanical methods, without the prior written permission of the publisher, except in the case of brief quotations embodied in critical reviews and certain other noncommercial uses permitted by copyright law.

Cover Design by WEMA Creatives.

Book Design by Saqib Arshad.

Printed in the United States of America.

First Printing, 2020

Unless otherwise indicated, Scripture quotations are from the New King James Version of The Holy Bible.

For permission requests to use the materials in this book, write to the publisher, at the address below.

DW Creative Publishers

4261 E. University Dr. #30-355

Prosper, TX 75078

www.DWCreativePublishers.com

connect@dwcreativepublishers.com

Dedication

My Daddy: You are indeed the LOVE of my life. I am extremely grateful. Without You, this would not be possible. I thank You for giving me the burden that led to this book. I also appreciate Your rebuke which really lit the fire to bring it to completion and for the grace to pen this first book. Thanks for all the inspiration You gave as I wrote. I am eternally grateful, Daddy. Thanks for loving me with an everlasting love.

To anyone who is seeking the Father's heart and has a desire to grow in deeper fellowship with Him, especially to those who have given up on prayer because of a failure to get answers.

To my late grandmother, Naomi Ralph, my first example of a life surrendered to God through prayer and obedience to His will for your life. Thanks for truly modeling a lifestyle of prayer for us. I am eternally grateful for the seeds you have planted.

To my sister, Ronell Purificato, my prayer is that in the fullness of time, you will fully walk in the plan of God for your life, carry on the legacy of prayer entrusted to our family and run your race well in the kingdom of God.

Acknowledgements

I am eternally grateful for the inspiration, wisdom and example of many amazing men and women who through their passion and obedience to God have allowed me to emulate them in some ways.

I am grateful for my pastor, the ministry I am affiliated with, my church family, especially the prayer team including my spiritual coverings (Randy and Nitra) whose prayers and support have been instrumental in this process.

For the development and production of this book, gratitude goes to:

- The core team of supporters for Women Who Love International, especially Aubria (sister) – thanks for always being supportive. I can always rely on your favorite response – "do it" to almost anything I decide to try. Special thanks to Marilyn, Erin, Marivel and Sylvia, for all your prayers, support, ideas, and feedback. I appreciate each of you so much!

- Sue Maynord and the Emerging Prophets School family, thanks so much for your obedience in prophetically declaring what was revealed to you regarding the birth of this book. There was no way you could have known I was contemplating writing a book except for the Spirit of God. Blessings to you and the entire EP family!

- My mom, Sylvia, I am eternally grateful for you exposing me to church at an early age. It was your "crazy" faith and your love for evangelism which helped to start my journey. Blessings to you!

- Danni W., my amazing editor and publisher: I am so grateful for you and the blessing you have been in bringing this first piece to life. I could not have asked for a more patient and diligent person. Daddy divinely connected us for this project, and it has been so easy working with you! Thank you.

Table of Contents

INTRODUCTION 1

CHAPTER 1: THE HAUGHTY LOOK 9

CHAPTER 2: A LYING TONGUE 19

CHAPTER 3: HANDS THAT SHED INNOCENT BLOOD . 29

CHAPTER 4 : A HEART THAT DEVISES WICKED IMAGINATIONS 39

CHAPTER 5: SWIFT TO DO EVIL 51

CHAPTER 6: A FALSE WITNESS THAT SPEAKS LIES ... 61

CHAPTER 7: HE THAT SOWETH DISCORD AMONG THE BRETHREN 67

CONCLUSION 73

Introduction

What you are about to read is the result of a nudge in my heart which started last year and was followed by some recent dialogue with God during which I sensed Him highlighting the following: while many profess their love for Him, they do not care enough to learn what He likes or dislikes. They keep gifting Him the things that they like, or the things that have not cost them anything. The problem with this is that the gifts do not always coincide with what He likes.

Think about it. How would you feel if someone keeps giving you gifts that you do not like? This is someone who is in a covenant relationship with you and continuously professes their love for you. As I answered that question candidly, I immediately said they most likely would not remain a friend for a long time. However, I realized the need to determine why a friend would continue to give me something which I had expressed disdain for.

The conclusions drawn were that they may have missed my declaration concerning that item (although unlikely since I am an over communicator), they may have misunderstood what I meant when I declared it, they may have heard a partial statement, or simply put, they never cared enough to remember because it is really about them and not about me. Do you have the tendency to love God on your terms? And do you love others solely based on how you desire to receive love? Let's look at the following scriptures to get some context on what loving God and others should look like.

"Teacher, which is the great commandment in the Law?" Jesus said to him, "You shall love the Lord your God with all your heart, with all your soul, and with all your mind." This is *the* first and great commandment. And *the* second *is* like it: "You shall love your neighbor as yourself." On these two commandments hang all the Law and the Prophets" (Matthew 22:36-37).

What amazing commands! We have been afforded an awesome privilege to honor these decrees of our Father. Sadly, many still do not really understand the implications of these commands, that love for God and humanity are the greatest achievements of this life. God designed us for relationship with Him and each other. As such it is imperative that we invest time in studying these commands and praying to the Holy Spirit for understanding and application of his command to love. Failure to do so is simply unwise and will always lead to our demise.

Our connection and obedience to God is critical in achieving strong relationships. It is no wonder that forming and maintaining healthy relationships are difficult for so many people. We are trying to love God and others on our own terms. We are ignoring and/or rejecting God's definition of love.

We are meant to connect with God. As we develop a relationship with Him, we learn about Him. We also learn what He requires of us to demonstrate love for Him and each other, our purpose in life, and how we fit in the purpose of each other's lives. This connection gives us insight into our daily experiences, from how we should respond in a conversation, where we should live, who we should intercede in prayer for to unplugging from social media. Yet, sometimes we can have intimacy with God and still lack a full picture of what He is doing. This is not because He is an elusive God who wants to confuse us, but because He is a loving Father who recognizes our human limits and seeks to protect us.

Recently, I felt an impression in my spirit and I was guided to the book of Genesis. I felt as though the Spirit of the Lord began to highlight that so many of us have never even considered

NAIDENE RALPH

His emotions when we think of the account of the fall of man in the Garden of Eden. We are often focused on Satan's deception of Adam and Eve which led them to disobedience (sin) against God and ultimately a separation from His presence. While it is important that we recognize and understand the entry point of sin in the world and its impact on humanity, we should also consider the heart of the Father.

Faced with the knowledge that the crown of His creation, the man whom He created in His image and likeness, the one He created to be His reflection in the earth, to dominate and rule on the earth as He does in Heaven had now become a victim of satan's devices; not only could I sense the brokenheartedness of the Father as He goes looking for the man already fully aware that he is no longer in view, but he is now hiding from His presence "amongst the trees of the garden." As the Father dialogues with the man who is now expressing fear and awareness of his nakedness, He knows too well that Adam has been exposed to another voice.

You see, fear and shame are inconsistent with God's character so the presence of this fear-shame duo was a clear indicator that Adam had sinned by disobedience to God's command. As a result, God deals first with the source of the sin and executes judgement on the serpent. He also pronounces judgement on Eve and Adam for their decision to violate His command. Despite the punishment they receive, we see equally the evidence of His love as He clothed their nakedness, because until then, Adam and Eve were fully clothed in His glory.

We can also recognize a display of the grace of God coupled with the truth of His Word. His love, while it is everlasting, is never just guided by emotions, but rather by decisions. He had already given Adam the consequence for eating of the **tree of the knowledge of good and evil** and because **He is not a man that He should lie** nor is He a God whose Words return to Him void, justice had to be served. As much as God loves His creation, like Adam, He has given us instructions to follow for our own protection. He has also provided redemption for our disobedience (sin) through the shed blood of Jesus Christ. However, when we violate His ways and choose to reject the sacrifice provided for us, we will remain in separation from Him and there will be an execution of justice. The wages of sin is still death.

No parent truly enjoys disciplining their children especially as it relates to punishment, but a good parent recognizes the importance of penalizing a child who continues to ignore the rules set in place for them. As the Good Father, God's intention is never to mismanage our lives. Built into every command given to us is a demonstration of His love and protection from the wiles of the enemy. However, we have an option to obey or not to obey.

The purpose of this book is to highlight the things God hates. If you find yourself violating His commands, intentionally or not, these things will cause a break in your connection with God. You see, to love God wholeheartedly is to keep His Words. It is deception to think that we can love God when we ignore and/or practice behaviors for which He has a strong disdain. Only when we discover and consistently apply the principles outlined in His Word, do we truly demonstrate our love for Him. When we are successful at doing this, we will simultaneously experience the joy of loving Him with every part of us, which in turn will allow us to truly love ourselves as His created beings. This will then compel us to love each other unconditionally, thus fulfilling the greatest commandment. Many times, we are attempting to "love" God and others based on a flawed perception of love. Since God *is* love, *any* attempt to love outside of His definition of love is already a farce.

My hope as you read this book and study the seven things God hates is that the principles and truths highlighted here will challenge you to examine your heart. If you discover that you are guilty of doing one or more of these things as I did while researching and receiving inspiration from the Spirit of God, I pray that your first step is to acknowledge your wrong and repent before God. If needed, reach out and apologize to anyone you may have hurt. Develop a hatred for these things that God hates and ask Him to turn your heart in the direction of His will. This will allow your connection with Him to be strengthened. You will experience a shift in your communication with Him and ultimately grow in your love relationship with Him and others.

Chapter 1
THE HAUGHTY LOOK

"When pride comes, then comes shame; but with the humble is wisdom" (Proverbs 11:2).

Then God said, "Let Us make man in Our image, according to Our likeness; let them have dominion over the fish of the sea, over the birds of the air, and over the cattle, over all the earth and over every creeping thing that creeps on the earth." So, God created man in His *own* image; in the image of God He created him; male and female He created them" (Genesis 1:26-27).

NAIDENE RALPH

Every manufacturer determines the value of his invention. For example, when you and I walk into a car dealership looking for a car, the price is most often displayed for us to see which is indicative of the fact that a pre-determined value has already been ascribed to the car. The onus is now on the buyer to ascertain whether they agree with the value and whether they will purchase it or not. If you proceed with the purchase, you are in fact validating the ascribed value and you are also indirectly agreeing to adhere to the instructions outlined in the operator's manual as it relates to operating and maintaining the vehicle. Adherence to the manufacturer's guide is critical for optimization and longevity of your car. Conversely, a choice to ignore the manual may result in abuse or mismanagement of your vehicle.

God, as creator or manufacturer of the universe has already pre-determined our value as His creation. Man was created in His image and likeness to reflect Him in the earth. He was pleased with His creation and called it "good." When we follow the narrative of creation, we see the fall of man and his disobedience to God which led to separation from God. However, we can also see the value of humanity to God when He was willing to lay down His life in order to redeem us to Himself. We can see further evidence of our worth to Him in **Psalm 8:4-6,**

"What is man that you are mindful of him, And the son of man that You visit him? For You have made him a little lower than the angels, And You have crowned him with glory and honor. You have made him to have dominion over the works of Your hands; You have put all things under his feet."

The fact that God chose to fashion all of us in His image is symbolic of our worth to Him. The notion that any human believes he or she is more valuable than another is not only contradictory to God's Word, but also perplexing. This incongruity with God's Word is rooted in pride. Scripture says that pride comes before a fall. Let's look at the evidence. In Genesis 3:4-6, we see Satan disguised as a serpent contradicting the command issued by God to the man (male and female). In so doing, he appeals to the woman's selfish ambition.

> **Then the serpent said to the woman, "You will not surely die. For God knows that in the day you eat of it your eyes will be opened, and you will be like God, knowing good and evil." So, when the woman saw that the tree *was* good for food, that it *was* pleasant to the eyes, and a tree desirable to make *one* wise, she took of its fruit and ate. She also gave to**

her husband with her, and he ate (Genesis 3:4-6).

Satan is successful in his plot to distort the truth, to seduce Eve and to lead both her and her husband into rebellion against God. He is ultimately successful in causing a separation between man and the presence of God which I believe was his overarching goal. Not only had his previous experience leading a coup in heaven against God positioned him well to expertly orchestrate and employ this strategy of deception, his current location on the earth was a result of his act of rebellion against God. Satan is in fact a certifiable witness of the end result for any being who opposes God's will or established order without yielding to His provision for salvation.

The Bible says in Isaiah 14:12-15: **"How are you fallen from heaven, O Lucifer, son of the morning! How you are cut down from the ground, you who weaken the nations! For you have said in your heart, I will ascend into heaven, I will exalt my throne above the stars of God: I will sit also on the mount of the congregation, on the farthest sides of the north. I will ascend above the heights of the clouds; I will be like the Highest. Yet you shall be brought down to Sheol, to the lowest depths of the Pit."**

Pride originated with Satan and continues to be one of the strongest weapons used to lead many into broken relationship with God and with each other. This is especially why God hates the very appearance of pride. Pride is also innately destructive which is why God *resists* the proud (James 4:6). This "haughty or proud look" is also evident in our tendency to ridicule and/or alienate what is different. It is a typical response for most who have never truly experienced the love of God and/or the love and acceptance that should come from our natural relationships.

All humans desire to be fully known and to be fully accepted for their uniqueness, yet many people fall prey to this ever-growing culture of bullying. Many are arrogant enough to think that others should adhere to their standards for acceptance. Those who do not fit the constructed societal norms whether in appearance, behaviors, or perspectives are often marginalized. The danger for those who practice bullying is that they have now exposed themselves to a condition of the heart that God hates.

It is possible to understand the mindset of superiority without applauding it. However, we live in a society where a failure to show support for popular perspectives and/or agendas are met with hostility. This culture purports a paradigm of self-worth or value in the context of financial status, academic achievement, physical appearance, careers, zip codes, and fame, among other things. The more you achieve in one or several of these societal benchmarks will determine your perception of self-worth and will naturally give rise to a "haughty look" towards those who have not attained as much as you.

Moreover, the standards within most of these elements used to determine value are always changing. At any given moment, you can experience a significant upgrade or worse, a total loss of value because of the arbitrariness of these standards. God intended for His creation to remain confident in knowing our self-worth is secure in Him and that security is firm since He is a God who does not change.

When we become victims of low self-worth through culturally imposed definitions, whether it is accomplished by systematic exposure to false images of significance or by the words of someone considered credible in our lives, the reality is that those prevailing thoughts are rooted in a spirit that is anti-God. These socially constructed definitions of a person's value are the enemies of our souls which constantly compete with the values that God has already determined for us. Not only do they threaten our ability to adopt "the mind of Christ" which sets our paradigms as it relates to our individual worth, it equally affects our ability to perceive the worth of those in our natural relationships well. The way we combat this spirit is by applying 2 Corinthians 10: 3-5: **"For though we walk in the flesh, we do not war according to the flesh. For the weapons of our warfare are not carnal but mighty in God for pulling down strongholds, casting down arguments and every high thing that exalts itself against the knowledge of God, bringing every thought into captivity to the obedience of Christ, and being ready to punish all disobedience when your obedience is fulfilled."**

Pride undoubtedly is the greatest kryptonite for humanity. Choosing to live in pride will always cause a rift in your relationship with God and others. However, humility will draw you closer to Him. God's desire for His children is that we walk in humility. Jesus modeled a lifestyle of humility and it is no wonder Jesus received public validation of God's pleasure in Him. He took delight in honoring God through a spirit of meekness by leaving His heavenly domain, not flaunting His kingship but exhibiting the lifestyle of a servant who mingled with people from every walk of life. Humility is a demonstration that we are submitted to the established will of God. In 1 Peter 5:6-7, we read the following: **"Therefore, humble yourselves under the mighty hand of God, that He may exalt you in due time,**

casting all your care upon Him, for He cares for you."

Based on this scripture, one may deduce that humility is not a natural response. And it is not! We can further qualify this position when we look at 1 Peter 5:5 in which we can see the command to "Submit." Thus, submission must in fact precede humility. If we are unwilling to submit to our elders and each other, then there is no point in proceeding to the next command to humble ourselves. Humility not only requires a denying of the flesh, but it demands intentionality and action. This is an opportunity for us to demonstrate what Paul implores us to do in Romans 12:1, **"present your bodies a living sacrifice, holy, acceptable to God, *which is* your reasonable service."**

When we take the posture of humility, we have an opportunity to be that "sacrificial lamb," knowing that even when our feelings may be justified, we will give up our right for the sake of peace. I also find the imagery in this scriptural reference riveting as I cannot help but picture an individual kneeling in submission before our Father who is standing with His mighty hand outstretched. If I am under His hand positionally, then it means that I have to reduce my frame considerably to fit. As such, I will be in an uncomfortable position, naturally speaking. Additionally, I have to remain there despite the discomfort until He determines that it is the proper time to lift me up from that place. He already knows that when my eyes are fixed on Him or as I behold Him, I will be transformed into His image from glory to glory (2 Corinthians 3:18) so by the time I am back to an upright position, a notable change would have occurred.

Many times, we abort God's desired positions and/or postures for us prematurely because we hate the accompanying discomfort. Giving up our right never feels good yet in doing so, we have an opportunity to please our Father and to be a light or a lamb to someone we may not consider deserving. In these instances, we demonstrate the Father's heart and set ourselves up for the same when needed. **"Knowing that whatever good any man does; he shall receive the same from the Lord...."** (Ephesians 6:8).

Beloved, if you recognize, as I did while writing this, that there are times when you are choosing not to walk in humility because you have not really understood the implications of your pride in those moments and the fact that you are dishonoring God, please pause here. Listen to the heart of the Father, simply acknowledge your wrong and repent.

NAIDENE RALPH
Let us PRAY!

Father, I thank You for speaking to my heart today. With lovingkindness, You continue to draw me to You. Father, I confess that I allow pride to dictate my actions many times and I know that it's Your will that I choose to walk in humility. You hate even a proud look because pride is of the devil and therefore does not exemplify You in any way. I ask You to forgive me for not considering You and Your desire in those situations because I was simply focused on my emotions and doing what was pleasing to me. Father, forgive me for also missing opportunities to demonstrate Your love to others as You continue to show me love even when I am undeserving. Even now, Father, open my eyes to see any pride in my heart and help me to humble myself before You. Father, I ask that You continue to turn my heart in the direction of Your will and strengthen me to honor Your will above my own so that You will be glorified through my life. Father, I release anyone who has hurt me, and I ask that You release me from any charges brought against me because of pride. Father, I thank You for Your amazing love and mercy toward me. I praise You for all You have done and will continue to do in and through me. In Jesus' name! Amen.

Chapter 2
A LYING TONGUE

"A lying tongue hates those who are crushed by it, and a flattering mouth works ruin"
(Proverbs 26:28).

Lying is commonplace in our culture today. It is as if there is an invisible decree backed by a compelling force to blur the line between falsehood and truth. This is evident in the rise of famous and successful people whose primary skillset is manufacturing impressive replicas of consumer products, be it knockoff handbags or jewelry among others. Equally popular, are artists who are gifted in transforming one's face and/or body to a preferred version of one's self.

Lies are deceptive by nature and the intent behind lying is to cause the hearer or viewer to believe something other than what is true. This deception can subsequently influence the hearer to decide against their better judgement which often results in their destruction and in some cases, adversely impacts those connected to them. This is the reason God hates a lying tongue.

> **"Therefore, putting away lying, "Let each one of you speak truth with his neighbor," for we are members of one another"** (Ephesians 4:25).

Lying can take on many forms including flattery, exaggeration, and withholding information. Flattery can be described as the act of giving excessive compliments to another motivated by a selfish heart whose goal is generally to gain approval with the recipient or even to take advantage of them. In the church, one can see evidence of flattery among the congregants with each other and even from leaders in the pulpit preaching messages that would win them favor with their audience.

> **"A man who flatters his neighbor, spreads a net for his feet. By transgression, an evil man is snared, But the righteous sings and rejoices"** (Proverbs 29:5-6).

According to the Merriam-Webster dictionary, exaggeration "is an overstatement of truth." People typically exaggerate because of fear, pride, or even self-pity. One common area where many people tend to exaggerate is on resumes. When seeking a position, people often resort to padding previous positions and at times, their academic achievement, with the goal of truly standing out among the pool of applicants. Along these lines, it is not uncommon for people who serve as references to represent a person's character as better than it is to assist them in landing a role. I have had at least two people who chose to disconnect from me for my failure to agree to serve as a reference for them as former colleagues. While I worked with them both, they were now applying for roles in which they had little or no experience but had restructured their resumes to align with the responsibilities required by the new role and desired that I corroborate their story. My refusal to agree was not understood or taken kindly as I appeared to be making a big deal out of a practice that everyone does. They simply wanted me to "help them out."

Another form of lying is withholding information, which is deliberately refusing to share pertinent information because the goal is to deceive. The person disseminating the information knows that if their audience has all the relevant pieces of data, they will most likely make a decision that is unfavorable to the sharer. There are so many examples of how failure to disclose pertinent information has resulted in many devasting circumstances. It has been the cause of many people losing homes in cases where a loan officer was not forthcoming about the full details of a loan offered to a homebuyer. It has been the cause of many failed marriages in which the couple who had entered a covenant relationship failed to disclose relevant information concerning their past and/or current life choices. These types of actions are certainly manipulative and should not be named among anyone who is a believer in the Lord Jesus Christ.

Undoubtedly, there are varying motives for lying. God hates lying because it is against His very nature. He is a God of truth and he has already determined what truth is for us. His Word is truth. Our enemy Satan is dubbed as "the father of lies." We see him in action in the book of Genesis using his deceptive strategy to mislead Eve and Adam, causing them to inadvertently lose the authority God entrusted them with. This behavior ultimately led to their removal from their domain, thereby impacting the entire human race.

Lies can have a devasting impact on the hearer and those who are connected to them. This is certainly evident in the aforementioned account of Satan's deception of Adam and Eve. When the serpent twisted God's command and planted a seed of doubt into the woman's heart, not only did she make a decision to disobey God, but she also encouraged her husband to participate in this act of disobedience and they both received the consequence of their decision. Their decision did not only impact them, but it affected the entire human race.

> **"Therefore, just as through one man sin entered the world, and death through sin, and thus death spread to all men, because all sinned—"** (Romans 5:12).

As for the perpetrator, he was also punished and received the consequence of his actions for deceiving Eve. We must remember every decision we make is a seed. If we choose actions that honor the Word of God, we will reap the rewards of that which is rooted in goodness. However, if we make decisions that dishonor the Word of God, we will reap those consequences as well, which will never have a good outcome for us. The harsh consequences of man's disobedience are demonstrated in Genesis 3:13-19:

> **"And the Lord God said to the woman, "What is this you have**

done?" The woman said, "The serpent deceived me, and I ate." So the Lord God said to the serpent: "Because you have done this, You are cursed more than all cattle, And more than every beast of the field; On your belly you shall go, And you shall eat dust all the days of your life. And I will put enmity between you and the woman, and between your seed and her Seed; he shall bruise your head, and you shall bruise His heel." To the woman He said: "I will greatly multiply your sorrow and your conception; in pain you shall bring forth children; Your desire shall be for your husband, and he shall rule over you." Then to Adam He said, "Because you have heeded the voice of your wife, and have eaten from the tree of which I commanded you, saying, 'You shall not eat of it': "Cursed is the ground for your sake; in toil you shall eat of it all the days of your life. Both thorns and thistles it shall bring forth for you, and you shall eat the herb of the field. In the sweat of your face you shall eat bread till you return to the ground, for out of it you were

taken; for dust you are, and to dust you shall return."

It is unnerving that lying is not only commonplace among society, but among the church community, especially followers of Christ. This is evident because most are not even bothered by their lack of integrity. Years ago, it was natural to trust people based on their word. If a person said that he or she would do something, you could take it to the bank. Not so today. From religious leaders to lay persons, the Word of God is even twisted to manipulate others or justify erroneous behaviors.

Lies are most often premeditated. The fact that we have an opportunity to ponder and carry out this plan makes this act very presumptuous, crafty, and intentional. Of course, there are moments when someone may lie out of fear, but regardless of the motive, God hates a lying tongue. If we really believe as Christians that the Holy Spirit lives inside of us, then how can we habitually lie to each other? In short, we are lying to the Holy Spirit.

Either we are truly ignorant of who we are as believers or we really do not believe God as we profess. Additionally, we may be bound by a stronghold that causes us to lie out of compulsion or we are just arrogant. When we read Acts 5, we can see a scenario when Ananias and his wife Sapphira chose to lie to the Apostles.

As Peter confronts Ananias, he clearly declared that Satan had filled his heart to lie. He further exposes that Ananias did not just lie to mere human beings but to the Holy Spirit. The outcome for this husband and wife was very severe – they died as a result. Thank God that He has not dealt with us in this way, but we are certainly always reaping the harvest from the seeds we sow especially when we fail to repent.

Friends, I must reiterate that God desires that we walk in truth. He is characterized by truth and as His children, we must emulate this trait and represent Him well. Not only is God pleased with a life of integrity, He rewards it. Here are a few scriptures concerning truth:

> John 4:24: **"God is Spirit, and those who worship Him must worship in spirit and truth."**
>
> 3 John 1:4: **"I have no greater joy than to hear that my children walk in truth."**
>
> Proverbs 11:3: **"The integrity of the upright will guide them, but the perversity of the unfaithful will destroy them."**

1 Peter 3:16: **"Having a good conscience, that when they defame you as evildoers, those who revile your good conduct in Christ may be ashamed."**

If you recognize that you struggle with integrity, this is God's nudge to You. He loves us and wants us to recognize that we were created to reflect His nature of truth. Here is your opportunity to acknowledge Him and repent.

Let us PRAY!

Father, I thank You that according to Psalm 119:130, the entrance of Your Word brings light and gives understanding to the simple. Thank You that according to Psalm 119:9-11, I can cleanse my ways by heeding to Your Word. As I seek You with my whole heart, let me not wander from Your commandments. Help me to hide Your Word in my heart that I may not sin against You. Father, thank You for reminding me that You hate lies. I confess that I have lied and struggle with lying. I ask You to forgive me for this violation against Your will and desire for me. I also ask You to forgive me for any damage I may have caused to anyone as a result of my lying. I forgive myself and I release any feeling of condemnation. Thank You that You are the Way, the Truth, and the Life and no one, including me, can come to You unless You draw us. Thank You for drawing me to Yourself today. I forgive and release anyone who has lied about me. I ask that You turn my heart in the direction of Your will. I declare that I now choose to walk in truth as this is honorable to You and because integrity and uprightness will preserve me according to Psalm 25:21. Father, I thank You for Your patience and love toward me. I bless You and praise You. In Jesus' name! Amen.

Chapter 3
HANDS THAT SHED INNOCENT BLOOD

"And He said, "What have you done? The voice of your brother's blood cries out to Me from the ground"
(Genesis 4:10).

From the very beginning of time, before there was any civil government in place, we can observe God in the book of Genesis legislating judgment on the first murderer, undoubtedly, demonstrating His disdain of murder. This is evident in the first account of murder as Cain kills his brother, Abel.

Cain and Abel were the first children of Adam and Eve. The scripture tells us that God favored

Abel's offering over Cain's. As a result, Cain was angry and invited his brother to a field, attacked and killed him there. After carrying out this vile act, he attempts to conceal it when God inquires of Abel's whereabouts. When he responds with a lie, God immediately exposes that his brother's blood was crying out from the soil suggesting that there can be no escaping the cries of innocent blood. As a result, Cain was punished for his crime of murder against Abel, as noted in Genesis 9:5-6:

> **"Surely for your lifeblood I will demand a reckoning; from the hand of every beast I will require it, and from the hand of man. From the hand of every man's brother I will require the life of man. "Whoever sheds man's blood, by man his blood shall be shed; For in the image of God He made man."**

When I think of those who shed innocent blood, I think of the number of babies aborted each year. Whose blood can be more innocent than theirs?

According to the WHO (World Health Organization), between 2010 and 2014, on average 56 million induced (safe & unsafe) abortions occurred worldwide each year. In the USA alone, the number of abortions performed in 2017 was 862,320, down 7% from 926,190 in 2014. Furthermore, the article states that "the abortion rate in 2017 was 13.5 abortions per 1,000 women aged 15–44, down 8% from 14.6 per 1,000 in 2014. **This is the lowest rate ever observed in the United States. In 1973, the year abortion became legal, the rate was 16.3%.**

There is no doubt that the topic of abortion is very controversial as there are many who believe it is okay to terminate a pregnancy up to a specific number of weeks because the fetus may not have formed yet. However, as believers, our stance must be driven by the Word of God. What does God really say about life?

When we look at Jeremiah 1:5, God is speaking to Jeremiah the prophet, and He tells him that before He formed him in his mother's womb, He knew him and ordained him to be a prophet to the nations. This tells us that none of us are accidents. Even though a parent may not have planned for the birth of a child, God already purposed for that child to be a part of His creation if He allows that child to be implanted in the womb of the mother. In John 10:10, Jesus says that **"the thief comes to kill, steal and destroy but He has come that we may have life and life more abundantly."** God is indeed the giver of life and life is very precious to Him.

NAIDENE RALPH

Another equally important issue today, are the accounts of African American deaths by the hands of police officers. In our nation, we continue to see headlines and reports of more police brutality against African Americans in videos depicting some of the most blatant evidence of a misuse of power. Not only are African Americans being killed by police officers, but there is hardly any accountability for their actions. Furthermore, many people seem to justify the victims' fate especially when he/she has had a tainted past.

This perception is so anti-American as the presumption of innocence is supposed to be one of the most sacred rights enforced by the justice system. An individual is presumed innocent until he or she has been found guilty by a court. The Fifth Amendment to the U.S. Constitution assures citizens that no one shall be "deprived of life, liberty, or property without due process of law." Yet, we are often confronted with evidence of a lack of due process as it relates to the African American community.

Police brutality against any race is wrong and there is strong evidence that supports that all cultures suffer harm including death from police officers. The reality is that there are more images and videos of police officers killing African Americans unjustly than any other group of people, so it is difficult to overlook this issue as some suggest.

Homicide, in general, is at a high rate in our nation. According to America's Health Rankings analysis by the U.S. Department of Justice, Federal Bureau of Investigation, United Health Foundation, and AmericasHealthRankings.org, in 2018, there were 16,214 homicides, or five homicides per 100,000 people. It almost appears that we have become so desensitized to the seriousness of taking another person's life that most people are not even moved to act when the victims are innocent.

In Exodus 23:7, God declares: **"Thou shalt keep thee far from a false matter, thou shalt not slay the innocent and the righteous: for I will not justify a wicked man."**

Furthermore, in Exodus 20, He states **"thou shalt not kill."**

In Isaiah 26:30, He says, **"Go, my people, enter your rooms and shut your doors behind you. Hide yourselves a little while until the wrath has passed."**

You may be saying as a believer that I have not killed anyone, but before you dismiss this, let's look at what Jesus says in Matthew 5:21-26 about murder:

> "You have heard that it was said to those of old, 'You shall not murder; and whoever murders will be liable to judgment.' But I say to you that everyone who is angry with his brother will be liable to judgment; whoever insults his brother will be liable to the council; and whoever says, 'You fool!' will be liable to the hell of fire. So, if you are offering your gift at the altar and there remember that your brother has something against you, leave your gift there before the altar and go. First be reconciled to your brother, and then come and offer your gift. Come to terms quickly with your accuser while you are going with him to court, lest your accuser hand you over to the judge, and the judge to the guard, and you be put in prison. Truly, I say to you, you will never get out until you have paid the last penny."

When we think of the aforementioned passage of scripture, it is important to filter this through the Holy Spirit who resides in us as a born-again believer. What is Jesus really saying here? Well, he is first confirming that the Mosaic law which states one should not kill is still relevant and that anyone who commits the act of murder will face judgement. The Pharisees were well-versed in the law and accepted that truth.

However, Jesus is also trying to get them to see that while murder is wrong and punishable, it is the heart that drives the action. This is what Jesus is more concerned with. Therefore, He adds that a state of anger towards another, insulting or demeaning another has the same consequences or judgement as the actual murder of that individual. Remember, thoughts lead to actions. **"For as a man thinks in his heart, so is he"** (Proverbs 23:7).

I do not know about you but having read that passage of scripture several times before, I really did not make the connection and had not pondered long enough to get the revelation, or the weight of the point Jesus makes regarding murder. With that in mind, I have been guilty of being angry with and insulting others numerous times without understanding the implications of those actions. I was therefore liable for the same judgment as someone who has committed murder. Wow! Thank God for His mercy and grace in allowing me time to come to this revelation so that I can walk in true repentance and receive His forgiveness.

Friends, God is more concerned about the condition and posture of our hearts before Him.

Every sin starts within the heart and this is the reason He admonishes us to **"keep our hearts with all diligence, for out of it spring the issues of life"** (Proverbs 4:23). Many times, we can do good works and for the majority of believers this is the measuring stick by which they evaluate their spiritual walk. But if the good we do is not motivated by love and a desire to honor Him beyond any natural pleasure or benefit that may be derived from that act, then we have missed the point. Or, as Jesus would say **"our righteousness does not exceed those of the Pharisees"** (Matthew 5:20).

If the Holy Spirit is speaking to you right now about the motives of your heart and/or He is highlighting someone you may be angry with or have treated poorly, then this is your opportunity to honor His presence and His voice to you. Remember, God is seeking those who will worship Him in Spirit and truth (John 4:23). Respond to Him today!

Let us PRAY!

Father, I thank You that You are a merciful God. I thank You that according to Psalm 119:130, the entrance of Your words give light and it gives understanding to the simple. Father, thank You for the privilege to come before You in repentance. I acknowledge that I have anger in my heart towards (Individual's name). Father, I ask that You forgive me. I release (Individual's name) and I forgive them as You have forgiven me time and time again. Father, release me from the judgement associated with violating Your precepts. Your word declares that if we confess our sins, You are faithful and just to forgive our sins and cleanse us from all unrighteousness. I ask You Father to heal my heart and any wounds this situation may have caused. Allow Your peace that surpasses all understanding to overwhelm me. Father, I receive Your forgiveness through the blood of Jesus Christ. As I reach out to (Individual's name), help me to govern my emotions well and allow me to choose words that are seasoned with grace. I also ask that You give me the grace to accept whatever the outcome is. In Jesus' name! Amen.

Please note that reaching out to the person may not always be possible. If the person is deceased or you no longer have access to the individual, still follow the prayer guide and know that God will forgive you. Release them and move on.

Chapter 4
A HEART THAT DEVISES WICKED IMAGINATIONS

"The heart is deceitful above all things, and desperately wicked who can know it?" (Jeremiah 17:9).

What is in your heart? To help us understand what I sense the Lord wants us to gather from this statement about His disdain for a heart that plots evil, we must define the heart as well as evil or wicked imaginations.

Let us start with a look at the heart. Naturally speaking, we know that the heart is an organ in the center of the circulatory system and functions as a pump to carry blood throughout the body. The Word of God tells us in Deuteronomy that life is in the blood, so undoubtedly the heart is critical to the life of an individual. However, when the scriptures speak of the heart, it is referring to the core of who we are which includes the seat of our thoughts, decisions, emotions, intelligence – the main frame of who we are. The heart is the engine of these vehicles we have been entrusted with to navigate this race course called life.

I find it interesting that the word heart which is *kardia* in the Greek (pronounced kar-dee-ah) is mentioned over 157 times in the Bible. This tells us the heart is clearly important to God thus it should also be important to us. Here are some key scriptures to keep in mind as we consider our Father's will concerning the heart of an individual.

In 1 Samuel 16:7, the scripture declares that while man looks at the outward appearance, God looks at the heart. In Matthew 22:37, **Jesus said unto him, "You shall love the Lord your God with all your heart, with all your soul, and with all your mind."** Proverbs 23:7 tells us **"for as he thinks in his heart, so is he."** And finally, in Proverbs 4:23 we read, **"keep your heart with all diligence, for out of it spring the issues of life."**

As I pondered the last scripture, I couldn't help but think of a few similarities to our physical heart. They are both hidden and not easily accessible. While the condition of the physical heart of a person is integral to the natural health of a person, the condition of the spiritual heart is critical to the spiritual health of that individual. Our natural diet can help or hinder the ability of the heart to carry out its original function. Likewise, our spiritual diet will determine the overall health of our spiritual hearts.

To have a healthy heart requires first an awareness of the implications of an unhealthy heart, followed by the knowledge of a daily regimen to foster a healthy heart. Even more, it requires application of that routine as well as periodic checkups to ensure that your program is actually producing the desired results. This checkup is often rendered by a professional who has the experience, and therefore, knows what to look for, how to diagnose as well as what changes to implement.

Similarly, we need frequent spiritual heart checks to ensure that we are aligned with the Father's definition of a good heart and we can only do so effectively, with the guidance of the Holy Spirit and the Word of God as the primary measuring sticks. Additionally, we can receive spiritual heart checks through spiritual leaders including Pastors, Teachers, and Prophets as well as through mature believers who can serve as personal mentors in our lives. We must also be willing to make the necessary adjustments if we are to have healthy spiritual hearts which are required in order to truly reflect the Father's heart. A failure to have those regular spiritual checkups can leave you in an undesirable position. The more consistent you are with "guarding your heart," the more successful you can be in preventing those heart issues and the more proactive you can be in addressing the issues that seep in unaware.

Now that we have established what encompasses the heart of a person and how our Father views us in light of the condition of our hearts, let's look at a definition for wickedness.

According to the International Standard Bible Encyclopedia, wickedness is defined as "a mental disregard for justice, righteousness, truth, honor, virtue; evil in thought and life; depravity; sinfulness; criminality."

From the beginning of time until now, God hates wickedness. While the use of the word "wicked" is most often reserved for those who have committed acts of murder, rape, and other actions we consider atrocious in our culture, it is important to note what God denotes as wickedness. Again, His definition is critical to us if we are to live a life submitted to the will of God.

The word "wicked" can be found about 115 times in the Bible. Here are a few key scriptures that confirm God's thoughts concerning wickedness:

As early as Genesis 6:5-6,

> **"Then the Lord saw that the wickedness of man was great in the earth. And that every intent of the thoughts of his heart was only evil continually. And the Lord was sorry that He had made man on the earth, and He was grieved in His heart."**

Later in 2 Chronicles 7:14,

> **"If my people who are called by My name will humble themselves, and pray and seek My face, and turn from their wicked ways, then I will hear from heaven, and will forgive their sin and heal their land."**

Finally, in Mark 7:21-23,

> **"For from within, out of the heart of men, proceed evil thoughts, adulteries, fornications, murders, thefts, covetousness, wickedness, deceit, lewdness, an evil eye,**

> blasphemy, pride, foolishness. All these evil things come from within and defile a man."

Friends, when we examine God's definition of wicked or evil, simply put, it is a disregard of His Word. This is usually evident in disobedience to His ways and choosing to do our own thing. Considering this, you will agree that we are in a culture similar to the one described in the book of Genesis. People are bent on disregarding truth and choosing what appears to be right in their own eyes. In the time of Noah, God became angry at the people's wickedness. **"Then the Lord saw that the wickedness of man was great in the earth, and that every intent of the thoughts of his heart was only evil continually"** (Genesis 6:5).

As a result of this, God said He was sorry that He had created mankind. He tells Noah, **"the end of all flesh has come before Me, for the earth is filled with violence through them; and behold I will destroy them with the earth"** (Genesis 6:13). When we read the entire account, we see that the earth is later destroyed by the flood; Noah and his family are the only ones who were preserved as a result of Noah's honor towards God.

Unfortunately, as a society, we are experiencing a very similar cultural setting. The "wickedness" of man is indeed great on the earth. People are obsessed with their own way of doing life and do not want to retain God in their knowledge. What is worse, is that this mindset is even prevalent in our churches. Many believers are so deceived, they have convinced themselves that God endorses their behaviors and/or choices because He wants us to be happy. If you fall into this category of believers who think this way, I hate to break it to you, but let's be clear, God is more concerned about His will being done in the earth over your personal happiness. If you have a hard time receiving that, please read the account of Jesus agonizing in the Garden of Gethsemane before He went to the cross. Jesus was not happy in that moment, and this is evident in His cry to the Father when He requested another way if it were possible. However, He chose to honor the will of His Father because He knew that our redemption was at stake.

In each of our individual journeys with the Father, there will be periods of discomfort and we will be required to give up some things we hold dear, be it relationships, careers, money, and/or opportunities for His sake. As a matter of fact, in Luke 9:23, Jesus declared that if anyone desires to come after Him, he must first deny himself, take up his cross daily and follow him. It is therefore deception to think that we can be true followers of Christ but are unwilling to deny anything for Him. And this unwillingness to obey Him is really an indication that we have bought into the lies of Satan who has at some point strategically infiltrated our minds to think that God is trying to keep something good from us. Like Eve in the Garden of Eden, who had access to *everything else* in the Garden except the tree of the knowledge of good and evil (which was only forbidden for their protection), Satan was successful in having her focus on the single prohibition versus the dominion, the authority, all the other trees and everything else that she had access to in her natural habitat. Not surprisingly, Satan still uses this strategy today. God has given us so many promises that are filled with His blessings if we obey, yet we often focus on what we are not allowed to do even with the negative consequences in view. The enemy of our souls wants us to disobey and forfeit not only the blessings already set aside for us, but he wants to destroy our relationship with God and cause us to also be disconnected from His presence. Satan has already lost his connection, his influence and his original position with God and he can never regain that so his goal now is to simply destroy our opportunity to be in and remain in God's presence.

Some people also believe that God understands when they plot and scheme to get ahead by using deception, even if it means highlighting another person negatively to gain advantage with a boss, or a relationship we are hoping to benefit from. Or, some believe that He understands when we just choose to continue in our sinful habits without repentance. After all, we are under grace, but is grace a license to continue in sin? God forbid! Does the grace of God mean that there is an automatic cancellation of the consequences of our actions even when we continue to violate His law? Absolutely not. There are many cases where Jesus demonstrates the love of the Father to those who were found infringing the laws, but He always cautioned them to "go and sin no more."

When we become born-again believers, it is only the beginning of our journey. It is imperative that we begin the work of sanctification which requires us to **"present our bodies as a living sacrifice which is our reasonable service"** and only then will we be **"transformed by the renewing of the mind"** as Romans 12 states. We must be intentional about this process; it requires our *active* participation.

When we accept the Lord Jesus as our Savior, our thoughts and actions are not automatically aligned with the Word of God. If we are unwilling to actively study the Word and regularly pray for the Holy Spirit's assistance to empower us to do what is written in the Word, then we may have experienced an act of salvation but will remain a carnal believer which means there is no change in how we lived before or after our supposed God encounter.

As believers, we cannot allow ourselves to live in constant violation of God's Word and think that we are still in fellowship with Him. Yes, we have a new covenant as believers and we are under the grace of God, but make no mistake, God expects us to live a holy life. Does that mean we will not miss the mark at times? Absolutely not. However, it should break our hearts when we miss the mark. It should make us run to our Father and ask for forgiveness. It should make us try our best to avoid repeating mistakes. What I am talking about is having a heart that is broken when there is a clear violation of the Word of God.

Friends, while God is always nigh to us, He is a Holy God and *will not* continue to reside in a vessel that is not set apart for Him. If you have found yourself in a place of living as a wicked servant, in violation of His commands and you find that the imaginations of your heart are evil continually, then here is your opportunity to invite the Holy Spirit to come in.

Let us PRAY!

Adonai, I thank You and praise You that You are a good, good Father! Father, as I hear your heart, I am choosing to respond to You. Lord, I acknowledge that I have been walking according to the dictates of my heart which is often in direct opposition to Your way. Father, I ask that You forgive me for my wickedness and that You create in me a clean heart and renew a right spirit within me. Remove my heart of stone and give me a heart of flesh. Father, I surrender to You afresh and ask that the eyes of my understanding be enlightened in the knowledge of You. Turn my heart in the direction of Your will. Help me to hunger and thirst for righteousness so that I will be filled. Grace me to hide Your words in my heart that I would not sin against You. Strengthen me Holy Spirit to honor You and to love You with all my heart, my soul and my mind and my neighbor as myself. Father, I thank You in advance for hearing and answering my petition today. In Jesus' name! Amen.

Beloved, while God indeed loves His children and desires that we are happy, He is far more concerned about His will being done in the earth.

Chapter 5
SWIFT TO DO EVIL

"Their feet run to do evil, and thy make haste to shed innocent blood; their thoughts are thoughts of iniquity; wasting and destruction are in their paths"
(Isaiah 59:7).

We live in an age of constant technological advancement where speed is everything. The ability to complete anything at lightning speed appears to be the goal of this age. While we can all appreciate the benefits of being the *first in time*, it has also brought some notable challenges. For the purpose of this chapter, I want to highlight the fact that our belief system has had to adjust to accommodate the emergence of a culture that equates speed with progress. As a result, this has affected some of the ways in which we process and deal with the issues in our lives even as it relates to our relationship with God and each other.

As followers of Christ, the Bible must remain the standard for us, even in a culture that is constantly evolving. The principles in the Word of God do not change with the times. We need to be constantly aware of this truth or we will be subtly lured into the changing tides only to find ourselves stuck in quicksand. God wants to remind us today that one thing we should not find ourselves racing toward is to do wrong, after all, He hates it.

When we talk about a race to do wrong or mischief, it is really addressing our response to the things that do not honor God. Our primary goal as believers should always be *to love what God loves and hate what He hates.* This requires us to know His Word and to be ready to apply it even when we disagree with it. His Word defines what is wrong and how we should respond in every situation.

Let us look at an example of a heart that was not quick to do wrong. Potiphar was Joseph's master who had entrusted the care of his household into Joseph's hands. Not only was Joseph successful in all that he did but we learn that he was well built and handsome. Potiphar's wife took notice of him and asked him to sleep with her. In

Genesis 39:8-15, we see his commitment to honoring God:

> "But he refused and said to his master's wife, "Look, my master does not know what is with me in the house, and he has committed all that he has to my hand, there is no greater in this house than I , nor has he kept back anything from me but you, because you are his wife. How then can I do this great wickedness, and sin against God?" So it was, as she spoke to Joseph day by day, that he did not heed her, to lie with her or to be with her. But it happened about this time, when Joseph went into the house to do his work, and none of the men of the house was inside, that she caught him by his garment, saying, " Lie with me." But he left his garment in her hand and fled outside. And so it was, when she saw that he had left his garment in her hand and fled outside, that she called to the men of her house and spoke to them, saying, "See, he has brought in to us a Hebrew to mock us. He came into me to lie with me, and I cried out with a loud voice. And it happened, when he heard that I lifted my voice and

cried out, that he left his garment with me, and fled went outside."

Look, all I know is that I want a heart like Joseph – where I fully count the cost of every decision I have to make and my greatest consideration would always be "how can I do this great wickedness, and sin against God?" You see in counting the cost Joseph was able to place his attention to all the great benefits that his master had afforded to him and in so doing recognize that the only prohibition was his wife. Joseph was successful in accomplishing what Eve (in the Garden of Eden) had failed to do when faced with a temptation and that was to count the cost. Note that choosing to honor God in a situation doesn't always mean that we would immediately see a reward for our obedience, clearly this is not how this account progressed. Oh, the lies that flowed from the lips of Potiphar's wife! I am taking some liberties here, but she sounds as if she had done this before or she had already contemplated her plan and determined how she would cause Joseph to suffer if he refused her. Remember the goal of the enemy is always to kill, steal and destroy. Either he will attempt to cause us to destroy ourselves through our disobedience to God or he will launch an assault on us when we do not take the bait. Yet in all of this, God's plan will prevail for those who flee even the appearance of evil and choose to honor Him.

How quickly we respond to the Word of God upon hearing it is indicative not only of our love for Him but of our understanding and revelation of His words. Joseph demonstrated his love for God verbally in declaring that he could not do something this wicked against God. We also see that love in action as he literally runs out of his cloak to avoid the advances of Potiphar's wife. His decision also displays love and respect for his earthly master as well as the role entrusted to him. This is really an unfolding of Jesus' commandment to love the Lord our God with all our heart, soul, and mind and our neighbor as ourselves. In choosing to love God first, he was able to love his neighbor (Potiphar). This is the type of heart that we all need to develop towards the Father and those around us.

Unfortunately, there is a loss of respect for the Word of God which is augmented by what I believe is the beginning of the **"famine for the hearing of the words of the Lord"** (Amos 8:11) as told by the prophet Amos. We are in a time when people are not enduring sound doctrine. Most people are ready to reject anything that does not involve them being happy. Additionally, we have now graduated to the "friend zone" with God. Because many people have a warped idea of what friendship is, we see this sort of casual response to the Word of God. God's commands are often treated as a recommendation or suggestion, after all, *nothing* can separate us from His love. There is seldom haste in applying the Word of God to our lives. As a matter of fact, I often find it very perplexing when I hear believers state they need to pray about doing something that God has clearly stated to do in His Word, yet I almost never hear those same people express prayerfulness about their regular indulgences such as eating, watching television, hanging out with friends, or taking a vacation. I would rather err or take a risk on doing something that is expressed in His Word which could have eternal impact (since according to 1 Corinthians 15:58, **when we abound in His work our labors are not in vain**) than to err or take a risk doing something that is driven by my flesh and will only reap temporary rewards, but that's just me!

Let us examine some situations which depict hearts that race to do wrong.

Divorce in our churches today is said to be equal in number to those in the world. This is not surprising when we evaluate the fact that most Christians and non-Christians approach marriage the exact same way. There is not much difference in our belief system. We choose our spouses the same way and for the same reasons and our objectives for marriage are the same. For many Christians, when marital issues arise, they are very quick to throw in the towel because they are convinced the goal of marriage is to make them happy along with all the other natural expectations they have. Everything we do is designed to bring glory to our God first and foremost, not to make us happy. I would argue that most often it is the opposite and we must be intentional about choosing to be happy, or rather *joyful*, despite our shifting circumstances.

Another thing I have noted is the race to be offended. This is like a virus in our world today. Not only are people easily offended, it appears that people enjoy finding opportunities to be offensive. We are quick to "clap back" and the faster you can do so, the wittier you are deemed. Respect is no longer a virtue. Today, you only get respect if you earn respect. While this may be true in the world, as children of God, we ought not to identify with this carnal mindset. We are quick to do everything the world does that it now appears the world has set the standard for the church, and we are left wondering why we have so much chaos in and around us.

Friends, as Christians, we now belong to the kingdom of God. This kingdom is governed by a theocratic system which means God decides what is wrong and right. We do not get to vote; our opinions are irrelevant. This is far from the democratic system of government which we as Americans have become accustomed to. As such, it behooves us to get acquainted with the kingdom of God if we expect to carry out God's will in a way that honors Him. He is pleased when we exercise self-control because that demonstrates His character in the earth. Being quick to do wrong shows that we lack self-control which means we need to be empowered by the Holy Spirit.

Let us PRAY!

Father, in the name of Jesus, I thank You that You are great and greatly to be praised. I thank You for Your love and for Jesus, who despite His agony in the Garden of Gethsemane, chose to honor Your Word over His emotions. In so doing, His sacrifice gives me access to Your grace and mercy and I am so grateful. Father, You said You hate feet that are quick to do wrong and I realize that I have found myself being quick to do wrong. Father, I repent of my_____ (name the wrong things you are quick to do). I ask You to forgive me for sinning against You and for hurting others (call the names of the specific people you've hurt) in the process. Father, please cleanse my heart and give me the grace and strength to be quick to honor Your Word instead. Fill me afresh with Your Holy Spirit to empower me to be an effective witness for You so that I can teach others to also honor You. Father, I thank You and praise You for Your Word because it's a lamp unto my feet and a light unto my path. Thank You for exposing this light to me today! I honor and praise You for all that You have done and all that You will continue to do. In Jesus name! Amen.

Chapter 6
A FALSE WITNESS THAT SPEAKS LIES

"No one who practices deceit shall dwell in my house; no one who utters lies shall continue before my eyes"
(Psalm 101:7).

The word *witness* is often associated with legal proceedings. This person is used to establish truth in a matter. Their role is typically giving evidence to confirm an event which took place and what was said or done. A witness' testimony can be critical to one's case and can essentially make or break you. As such, for court proceedings, many lawyers spend time vetting potential witnesses to ensure they will truly add value to their client's case. It is not uncommon for a lawyer to opt to not put a witness on the stand especially when their character is not laudable as this can jeopardize the effectiveness of their testimony.

I think it is interesting that the Word of God states **"... In the mouth of two or three witnesses, let every word be established"** (2 Corinthians 13:1). Before we arrive at any conclusion or decision in a matter, we should have at least two people corroborating an account. Too often, we are concluding a matter without enough supporting evidence.

In Proverbs 6, we learn that God hates a false witness who pours out lies. We have talked about the seriousness of serving as a witness in which the overall goal is to establish truth. Therefore, when we think about a false witness, the implication is that the individual was not a part of the event or situation they are willing to substantiate. Additionally, it means they must plan, create, and execute the narrative with which they hope to persuade their audience.

You may be saying, I would never do something like that. You see, we may not go to a court of law and serve as a material witness knowing we would pay a steep price if it were discovered we were intentionally falsifying information to mislead the jury. However, we may have shared our side of a dispute we experienced and exaggerated (lied) to make it appear that we were in the right and the other person was horrible to us. Your account may have caused the person or persons listening to you to have a shift in perspective regarding the other person in your story. Or, you may have shared some key pieces of embellished information with a boss "out of concern" for a coworker when your goal was simply to highlight yourself or to be noticed. Maybe you served as a reference for a friend or family member who you know is "shady" or a better phrase is "they are still being processed" and you would not hire them if you had a company. However, you were willing to give a stellar review to their potential employer. After all, your goal was just to help them get a job, no harm in that.

Or maybe you have served as a good friend to someone who found herself in some trouble because she lied to her authorities about her whereabouts and told them that she spent the night with you. As her friend, you felt as though you had no choice but to protect her, so you confirmed her story knowing you had not even seen her that night.

Friends, we live in a time when the lines between truth and lies are extremely blurred. We live in a culture saturated with fake news, photoshopped photos, and filters. Authenticity has become quite rare. The enemy of our souls has craftily developed an environment which thrives on falsehood. What matters most is how good you are at selling your narrative even if it is untrue. Unfortunately, many believers have fallen prey to this mindset and even in our lives we are practicing illusionists.

Furthermore, many of us are so desensitized and totally oblivious to these subtle but targeted plots of the enemy that we don't even realize we are engaging in behaviors that our Father despises. Or, we make excuses for our sins or justify them, and in some cases, we no longer feel the conviction of the Holy Spirit. Yet, we are still convinced we are good with God and continue in our daily religious activities of service to God.

Let us be clear that God, the Creator of this universe who set the world in motion by His words, who displaced Satan and those he led in rebellion against God from heaven, who drove Adam and Eve outside the Garden because of their disobedience to God, ensured punishment which led to a break in fellowship between man and His creator.

Yes, I hear you even now saying, but this is the law; we are in a dispensation of grace. You are correct. Yet Adam and Eve's outcome occurred before the law was given and they reaped the consequences of their actions. Jesus said, I am not come to destroy the law but to fulfill the law.

Moreover, Jesus said in the gospels, a new commandment I give to you, love the Lord Your God, with all your heart, soul, and mind and your neighbor as yourself.

If our command is to love Him with everything, how can we genuinely love Him but continue to do what He hates and think we are maintaining good fellowship with Him? Even in our natural relationships, we would not continue to remain close friends with anyone who is bent on doing those things we have expressed dislike for.

God is letting us know that to be a false witness who lies is absolutely something that He hates. It does not line up with His nature or character and should not be a part of our lives if we are living a life surrendered to Him. When we operate in falsehood, we are operating in the kingdom of darkness because Satan is the father of lies. This practice aligns with his nature. Furthermore, when we stand as a false witness and lie on another individual, not only can their reputation be tainted but it can have a devastating impact on the lives of their family members. In these instances, you are also not loving your neighbor as yourself and therefore not fulfilling the command of the Lord.

If you can identify an operation of falsehood in your life, here is your opportunity to thank the Lord for highlighting that issue, for giving you a chance to repent and renounce this behavior of sin. If you are not sure, just ask the Holy Spirit to reveal in your heart any area where you may have served as a false witness and He will show you if something is there.

Let us PRAY!

Father, thank You so much for Your Word to us. Thank You for showing me the error of my ways. Father, You said if Your people who are called by Your name will humble themselves and pray, turn from their wicked ways, You will hear from heaven and You will heal their land. Lord, I confess that I have walked in a way that is displeasing in Your sight. I ask You to forgive me, Father, for being a false witness and for any damage I have caused to others because of my actions. I thank You that You have already made provision for my sins through the blood of Jesus Christ. I receive and I accept your forgiveness. I apply the blood of Jesus over my mind to purge these dead works of the flesh. I declare that I walk in truth because You are the Way, the Truth, and the Life. I thank You for Your grace and mercy. I ask that You continue to transform me into the image of Your dear Son, Jesus. I honor and praise You. In Jesus' name! Amen.

Chapter 7
HE THAT SOWETH DISCORD AMONG THE BRETHREN

"Do not be deceived, God is not mocked; for whatever a man sows, that he will also reap. For he who sows to his flesh will of the flesh reap corruption, but he who sows to the Spirit will of the Spirit reap everlasting life. And let us not grow weary while doing good, for in due season we shall reap if we do not lose heart"
(Galatians 6:7-9).

Having grown up in a predominantly agricultural society, I am immediately drawn to the verb "soweth." In Matthew 13:1-23, Jesus talks about the sower, the soil, inhibitors to the growth of the seed, and the reaping process. In this parable, we learn that the seed is the Word of God and the soil is the hearts of men. I find it interesting that King Solomon would use this same verb in the Old Testament to express God's heart as it relates to the topic at hand.

I suppose He ultimately desires to shift our paradigm to adopt the mindset of a sower. We are all sowers whose greatest currency are the words that we deploy. The words we speak are seeds and they will one day yield a harvest if they fall on the right soil and are nurtured over time. I think it is fair to say that we all have a good grasp of the principle of sowing and reaping as it relates to an investment of our time, treasure, and talents. However, we seem to quickly dismiss or discount this principle when we engage in negative behaviors. I believe this is the reason the Apostle Paul in Galatians exhorts us to not be deceived for "whatsoever a man sows that shall he reap." It is deception to think we do not reap a harvest when we sow bad seeds.

In Proverbs 6, we learn that God hates when one sows discord among the brethren. Discord is a weapon in the enemy's arsenal and should never be deployed by a person who is surrendered to the Lordship of Jesus Christ. This weapon of the enemy is widely used in every facet of our society today. It has led to the destruction of marriages and friendships, the severance of business relationships and church splits as well as projects being derailed among many other things.

In John 17, a chapter I consider very essential for every believer, as Jesus is praying to the Father, He gets ready to return to the Father. He is praying for all who will believe which includes us today and His petition is that all believers would be one as He and the Father are one. This oneness is critical for believers because it should be our brand of authenticity. We should strive daily for this feat as a corporate body because it is Jesus' desire for us. This oneness will also serve as an impetus for the world to believe that Jesus was sent by the Father. With this in mind, it is fair to deduce that as long as the church or professing followers of Jesus Christ remain divided, chances are the world will remain polarized from a belief that Jesus indeed came in the flesh.

We can clearly understand the Father's hatred of sowing seeds of discord or division. Not only does it yield a return of division in so many aspects of our lives, it is also the reason in Matthew 12:25, Jesus declares every kingdom divided against itself is brought to desolation, and every city or house divided against itself will not stand. Furthermore, we can see the implications for those who are outside the kingdom of God.

The Word of God also tells us that we are not ignorant of the enemy's devices.

The psalmist David tells us that it is good for **"brethren to dwell together in unity."** God *delights* in unity. The success of any organization, team, family, or relationship is directly related to our understanding of unity and our ability to function in harmony. Unfortunately, in our culture, strife is the order of the day. Negativity spreads like wildfire and people seem to have a strong affinity for anything that creates division. Now more than ever, God expects His children to come to a place of understanding His will for the church, what true identity and authenticity mean, how to walk in maturity, and how to partner with Him to mobilize a movement of preparedness for a great end time harvest.

Beloved, as you take a moment to reflect, ask the Holy Spirit to show you where you have been a sower of discord and as He highlights these areas, take ownership and repent of making decisions to operate in this way.

Let us PRAY!

Father, I thank You for Your Word which is a lamp to my feet and a light to my path. I thank You for the opportunity to hear Your heart and to learn more about You today. I confess that I have sown seeds of discord and I ask You, Father, to forgive me for not honoring Your Word. Father, Your Word declares that if we confess our sins You are faithful and just to forgive our sins and cleanse us from all unrighteousness. I thank You that I have access through Jesus Christ for the remission of sins and therefore through faith, I receive Your forgiveness. Father, I release anyone who has hurt me, and I ask that You release me from anyone who has an ought against me. I declare that I have the mind of Christ and I am being transformed into the image of Jesus Christ more and more each day. I confess that I love unity and promote peace. I declare that I am a peacemaker and take pleasure in honoring Your Word in my life so that You receive all the glory and praise. I thank You for answering my prayer today. In Jesus name! Amen.

Conclusion

When we look at the nations of the earth today, we are undoubtedly in unprecedented times. There is chaos everywhere and everyone is impacted. Even now, much of what we have grown used to is changing quickly. I can hear the echo of all creation groaning for redemption (Romans 8:22). The earth is travailing more than ever before. There are birth pangs everywhere and something notable is on the horizon. Many people are despondent, some are hoping that this whole year will just spring forward into 2021, some are trying to keep hope alive, others are strong in their faith, some are now emerging into an awareness of their own humanity and are open to the idea of God, some are questioning their belief in God, and others are trying to determine where God is in all of this.

The Word of God tells us in John 1:17 that **"grace and truth came through Jesus Christ."** It was meant to be like Siamese twins who are almost never separated because of how joined together they are. We have all received full access to the grace of God and it is His grace that allows us the confidence to walk in the truth of His Word. When we dwell more on the grace of God without truth, it is no wonder we have produced a culture that understands grace but rejects truth. We can believe God loves us but are not compelled to change our behavior or abandon our sinful ways. We can believe we sincerely love God, but do not think we need to demonstrate this love which most often requires a sacrifice as Jesus modeled for us.

Yet in God's lovingkindness He wants us to be aware of the things He hates and gives us an opportunity to respond. Recently, I recall my pastor sharing a message about parenting. He stated that it was unfair for a parent to punish a child for something they have not taught them.

I believe that it is the Father's desire as a parent to highlight these *seven* things that He hates for His children because some are not aware, some have forgotten, and some just do not think these apply anymore. Remember, **God decides** what is right and wrong in His kingdom. As believers, we are called to love the Lord with all that we are as well as our neighbors. When we examine the things God hates, it impacts our relationship with Him and others. Our horizontal and vertical relationships are interdependent. To be effective in these relationships, we must be yielded to the Holy Spirit and apply what He has written in His Word. God is counting on us to demonstrate His love in the earth; many are still waiting to see an expression of His love. He is counting on you to demonstrate your love for Him in the manner that He has expressed in His Word which also means you have to consider what He **hates.**

Bibliography

"Exaggeration." *Merriam-Webster*, Merriam-Webster, www.merriam-webster.com/dictionary/exaggeration.

"Preventing Unsafe Abortion." *World Health Organization*, World Health Organization, 26 June 2019, www.who.int/news-room/fact-sheets/detail/preventing-unsafe-abortion.

"Wickedness - International Standard Bible Encyclopedia." *Bible Study Tools*, 1915, www.biblestudytools.com/encyclopedias/isbe/wickedness.html.

America's Health Rankings analysis of U.S. Department of Justice, Federal Bureau of Investigation, United Health Foundation, AmericasHealthRankings.org, Accessed 2020. https://www.americashealthrankings.org/explore/annual/measure/Crime/state/ALL

Made in the USA
Coppell, TX
03 August 2020